Money For Retirement

The Middle-Aged Man's Survival Guide

By

Zackary Richards

Disclaimer

Money for Retirement-The Middle-Aged Man's Survival Guide was written by Zackary Richards

Published by Ari Publishing

This book makes no guarantees that by following the instructions outlined you will create additional income for retirement. There are many factors involved when it comes to earning additional income. The niche selected, the amount of time and effort put in, the present market etc.

What this does is show how the author and others were able to earn money for retirement by utilizing the outlined methods. Your results may vary.

Why Earning Additional Income for Retirement is Important

I distrust anybody who thought school was a good time. Anybody.—

Stephen King

I'm going to cut to the chase. In this book I'm going to teach you how to make a passive income that should steadily increase your monthly earnings to the point where you won't have to be concerned about money in your golden years. There will be nothing complex. Nothing to make you throw in the towel and say this money-making business is just too difficult to understand.

It really isn't.

Banking and finance people just want you to think it is so you will give your money to them to "properly manage it for you."

For a reasonable fee of course.

Quite a few of us lost our savings and investments during the Great Recession and it became pretty obvious that these financial professionals had no more idea of what to do during that emergency than we did. So many of us were nearly wiped out that a considerable number are filing for Social Security on their 62nd birthday. And with good reason. As I learned the hard way after I was downsized, nobody wants to hire a guy over 50—unless of course you are a member of upper management.

What they wanted—and still want—are indentured servants. College grads who are drowning in students loans and need a job, any job, just to keep from going broke. They live in their parent's basement (very likely yours) and are working two and three part-time minimum wage jobs. They are bright, energetic and are convinced that their hard work will be rewarded with promotions and salary increases.

Once they realize they are making other people rich while getting none of the benefits of their hard work, they request a raise or promotion and are summarily fired and replaced with another desperate young person trapped in the same difficult situation.

And this situation is not going to change as long as those in power have anything to say about it. Why? Because the stock market is at its highest point ever and Wall Street is once again making huge amounts of money. Such perks as employer health care, 401K's and pensions have all but dried up. There is virtually no interest paid on savings accounts and what value your money does have is devalued by 3% a year due to inflation.

In addition, huge sums of money are being invested in 3D printers and advanced technology like the Watson computer. And because of this, most manufacturing and service jobs will be obsolete in the next few years.

And because the wealthy own most of the media, they accuse the unemployed or under employed as being lazy and wanting to live off the backs of those working so hard to make ends meet. The truth is these people are eliminating more jobs than they are creating.

It's an old trick. <u>According the U.S.1860 Census, when slavery was at its peak, only 1.6% of the American population owned slaves</u>, yet that 1.6% were able to convince the southern white population to fight and die for a system that kept white working class wages low and the competition for jobs high.

And keep this in mind. There are political candidates with considerable financial support and a growing number of followers who are calling for the end of both Social Security and Medicare, claiming they are entitlement programs even though you have been paying into them your entire working life.

And that's why you need this book. **Because that _can_ happen**. How? Well just promise those desperate college grads who are just one paycheck away from being homeless that they won't have FICA taking such a big bite out of their weekly paycheck anymore. For them, retirement is 40 years away and they need money _now._ You Gramps, will have to fend for yourself.

Here's a look at the financial trouble our young people are in. The average income for those who actually have a real job is $46,000 dollars a year. So let's look at an average couple with one child.

Monthly gross income: $3833.33

Federal tax	$324.71
Social Security	$237.67
Medicare	$55.58
State tax withholding 5%	=$191.00
Net Income	$3024.37

Now let's deduct <u>monthly</u> expenses.

Rent or mortgage	-$1000.00
Home owner insurance	-$350.00
Utilities	-$200.00
Food	-$350.00

Car insurance	-$100.00
Cable TV, internet and cell phones	-$150.00
Car payment	-$300.00
Gas	-$120.00
Student loan	-$280.00
School costs or Daycare	-$150.00
Total=	**-$3000.00**
Balance	**$24.37**

And this is a conservative estimate. When has a month passed without some unexpected expense? A doctor's appointment, a visit to the dentist or the vet or a new car battery or a new computer.

As Roseanne Roseannedanna used to say "It's always something."

This bring us back to Stephen King comment. To this day I can't think of a single thing I learned in high-school that has had any practical use. Even English grammar, which I use to peddle my trade as a writer, was taught in middle-school. In high school I was taught Latin and French, Algebra, Geometry, Trigonometry, and Calculus. American and European history, biology, earth science and English Lit.

Although I strongly suspected at the time that everything I was being forced to learn was an incredible waste of my time, they warned me that if I didn't buckle down and study that stuff, I wouldn't be able to get a good job and would wind up broke and homeless.

I realize now that what I was really being taught was to be subservient and to subjugate myself to the needs of the wealthy and powerful. Don't believe that to be true? Then ask yourself why the one subject that was absolutely essential to my success and happiness was never taught. What am I talking about? I'm talking about how to make money, how to invest, how to buy property, how to start a business, how the economy works and how I could become financially independent.

Those are skills necessary for everyday life. If they taught those skills in middle or high school, I wouldn't need to spend money on college. I wouldn't need to put in long hours at a job I didn't like. I wouldn't need to struggle with money issues all the time.

Because I WOULD KNOW how to make all the money I needed.

Here's something else they never told you. In order to make money, you need to learn **how** to make money. How many times were the words, "Get a good education so you can get a good job." drilled into you?

Translation: *Learn to do something that a wealthy person can access so they can pay for that access until the time they can get it cheaper from someone else or no longer need it due to advancing technology.*

Just how in blazes does that benefit you? Just how do you come out on top in that scenario?

Even though we are in the 21 century we still have the antiquated notion that rich people are somehow smarter or better than we are. I know several wealthy people and no, they are neither smarter nor better. They simply looked around and saw how the world really works. Not that fairy tale version that if you work hard and play by the rules you will be amply rewarded.

What they saw was this.

Money = Influence = Power

Then they saw that to get money you only needed to find out what people wanted, get it, and then sell it to them at a profit.

Too often when people are told this they say, "It can't be that easy."

Actually, yes it is. And the reason people do get rich is that they get out of their comfort zone, find out what people want, sell it to them and make a profit. Then they find out what else people want and sell them that too.

Soon they are selling so much that they need help. So they hire people who are supposedly very smart, with advanced degrees, to help them sell. And as long as the person they hired continues to be profitable to their business, they are employed.

Do you think Old Joe Kennedy told his kids to get an education so they could get a good job working for somebody else? I strongly doubt that. I feel quite confident in saying that Old Joe told his kids to get a good education in business and politics, so kids like me who were learning Latin and Trig, could grow up and devote their lives to making them even wealthier.

Now let me point out that I do not begrudge them that education, because frankly I didn't know it existed. My parents didn't know it existed and it's very likely my grandparents didn't know it existed. Like them, I grew up working class. I was expected to graduate, get a job, work until retirement and then live off my savings, my pension and Social Security

It didn't work out that way. My pension disappeared when the company went bust, my savings dried up during the Great Recession and according to that Social Security letter I receive every year, my benefits won't cover my expenses.

Fortunately, I learned how to make money and no longer need any of those things.

In time it's likely you won't either. However I am legally obligated to inform you that you may not make any money at all. For example, I could teach you exactly how to repair any automobile but even if I did, there is no guarantee that if you opened an automobile repair shop, you would get customers and make a profit.

However, there is a far greater chance of you turning that repair shop into a profitable business with training, than without it.

I also need to point out that what I am going to teach you is no get-rich-quick scheme. Like any business model it will take some time to fully understand what works and what doesn't, as well as a commitment to making it a success.

If you're suffering from "Old Dog, New Tricks" syndrome, this likely won't work for you.

Starting out I had far more failures than successes. This is primarily because the people teaching these methods were marketers and were determined to keep me in the dark as a customer as long as possible.

That is not the case with me. By trade I'm a writer and that's how I make my money. I market my books, videos and various affiliate products. For example: On one of my websites I sell a gun that shoots table salt to kill flies mid-air.

I generally market it around Father's Day and get a good number of sales because it's a unique gift and shows that some thought was put into it.

I'm also going to dispel a number of myths when it comes to using the computer to make additional income.

First of all, making money on the Internet is not a scam or a rip off, although there have been instances where the inexperienced have lost some money paying for products that are utter crap and not worth a dime.

What most people fail to understand is that the Internet is now the largest marketplace in existence. Amazon is an online company that sells in the billions. So is eBay, Netflix and iTunes and thousands more.

I know from my own experience that there are hundreds of different ways to make money on the internet and the best thing about it is that most of that money is passive income. Internet businesses are open 24/7 and with each sale a commission check gets sent to your PayPal account or to your home if you prefer.

Basically that is all there is to it.

Another thing that drives people away from online income is that they think it's too difficult to do. That they need to learn computer coding and web design to create a website. No you don't. The truth is you don't need to spend time creating websites and writing content. Those who make big money on the internet don't. They outsource that to www.fiverr.com and www.iwriter.com/ . For less than twenty dollars you can have a complete website up and running in a day or two.

But I'm getting ahead of myself. And that's the one thing that is dangerous about making money online. People become overwhelmed by having so many options that they want to try them all and wind up not making a dime.

Another concern people have is that hackers will break into their computers and steal their pin numbers and credit cards and banking information. Here is a fact. It is far more likely that your credit card information will be stolen at a local restaurant or retail store than online. In addition, hackers generally aren't interested in small websites. Still, it's always a good idea to protect yourself so make sure your computer has a strong anti-virus/hacker protection. I use a free program called www.avast.com Another option is to download any and all financial information from your computer to a flash or thumb drive. This way your personal information will not be on your computer yet easily accessible by simply inserting the flash drive into the computer's USB port.

Here's the gist of it. If you keep the process very simple, and do what I outline one at a time, you will see how and why the process works and will likely start seeing some income (a little at first) that can grow larger as you become better at it.

Another advantage is that getting good doesn't take long. You can make a steady income putting in only a few hours a day. And yes, there is a better than average chance that you could retire early.

In order to succeed you will need to create a positive mindset.

Let's begin with this. You can't be truly happy or successful without creating a positive mindset.

And... just like that I've made a few enemies.

Still, it doesn't make what I said any less true.

I understand people don't like being told what they can and cannot be. People believe *they* decide if they are going to be happy or not and they don't need any hippie-dippy, touchy-feely new age nonsense, especially from a guy they don't even know.

That's what many people believe, but as much as they want to believe it, it's not true.

You will never be truly happy or successful until you create a positive mindset.

I've spent four decades of my life with a negative mindset. Often feeling unhappy and unappreciated. But the truly saddest thing about that was that it didn't have to be that way. I could have easily turned it around...

But... I didn't know how.

And most people don't know either. That's why I included this chapter in a book about money for retirement. And if you read it and follow through with the instructions given, you will likely be somewhat amazed at how the quality of your life improves.

I certainly was.

Still skeptical? I don't blame you. Like I said it does sound like a bunch of hippie-dippy, touchy-feely nonsense but it's not. The problem is that people are afraid to accept that reality because it means they likely wasted the better part of their lives being unhappy and unsuccessful.

That certainly was the case for me.

This is not to say I had a miserable life. Or that I was constantly depressed and withdrawn. Not at all. You see, generally I'm a pretty positive person. And I've accomplished a lot because of that positivity. The only thing I regret is that I could have accomplished a lot more if I had created a positive mindset instead of a negative one.

Why a negative one? I believe it goes back to my going to a Catholic Grammar and High School. I received a pretty good education but I also received some very damaging indoctrination that skewed my thinking for decades.

We were taught that we are all sinners and we must always be repentant and self-effacing. For example: If you thought that something you created was pretty good, that was the sin of pride. If you were pissed that someone beat you at some game or something that was jealousy. If you liked eating, that was gluttony. If you wanted to be rich, that was greed, and so on. And on top of it, these were all mortal sins. Sins you went to hell for.

Holy Crap!

It wasn't until I was older that I discovered that beat-you-down mentality was the norm, not just a Catholic school construct. A good friend of mine who grew up in a rural environment said he was always told "Don't forgit yer raisin'" Which translated means: Don't forget how you were raised or don't try to be anything more than you were raised to be.

Another thing we were all taught was that we needed to get a good education, so we could get a good job…

Working for someone else.

So let's have another look at that.

Psychologically what you're being told is that you aren't smart enough or good enough or clever enough to build a business of your own. The best you could do was to humble yourself to your betters, and do as they told you. And this type of information was passed down from generation to generation.

So that's what I did because I didn't know any better. I got a good education, and got what I thought was a good job and did as I was told.

And I was utterly miserable.

You see, I'm not a 'day person'. I don't get hungry until about three in the afternoon. I'm a creative person, not an analytical one. With very few exceptions I was a lot smarter than my bosses. And when I would point out how they could do the job more efficiently, and less costly, instead of being rewarded, I was targeted and reprimanded. Because this often cost me my job, I quickly learned to keep quiet, play office politics, and keep my head down.

So how can you, me or anyone be happy and successful in that kind of environment?

Plain and simple, you can't!

So over the next few pages I'm going to show you how you can create a positive mindset. And the reason why, is because I want you to succeed. Too often I've seen people with a real potential to make a very good passive income, give up because they ran into a setback or two.

What I'm teaching here is real business. And like all real businesses it will require time and effort to succeed. And most of all it will require a positive mindset.

The first thing you need to know is that your brain functions very much like a computer. This is a proven scientific fact. You subconsciously become whatever you tell yourself you are.

For example, if you are constantly berating yourself for mistakes or missteps and say things like, "I'm such a screw up", or "Everything I touch turns to crap", or "I'm so stupid," what you are doing is programming your brain to carry out those beliefs. So when you reach a critical juncture in any important goal you're working toward, your subconscious will cause you to overlook an important step or forget a necessary skill or any number of things that will ensure the end result will be failure.

Why?

Because that's what you programmed your brain to do. You are sabotaging yourself with such self-recriminations and you will not succeed until you stop and work toward developing a POSITIVE mindset.

I'll give you an example. You've heard of Thomas Edison. During his very successful career he announced that he was going to invent the electric light bulb.

Time passed with no results however and a reporter asked him how he felt about failing to create the light bulb. To which he replied, "I haven't failed. I've simple discovered ten thousand ways that don't work."

Do you see the absolute refusal of failure? The iron-clad belief that success was just around the corner? That is a positive mindset.

So how do you acquire that mental attitude? You start by beginning each day by watching one video on YouTube on *Positive Thinking and Motivational Thinking.* There you will find videos from people like Tony Robbins, Zig Ziglar, Jim Rohn and Dr. Wayne Dyer. Find the ones that speaks to you and watch them over and over for one month.

If you are a student of the lives of successful people like I am you will see they all have the same trait of thinking positively. They accept failure as just a necessary component of creating a successful venture. They don't bemoan cruel fate, or failed projects, or setbacks. They simply make a note of what went wrong and train themselves to avoid making that same mistake again.

Life is filled with bitter people who will dismiss your plans and desires for success as foolish and impossible. Why? Because misery loves company. Nobody likes to be miserable yet when it strikes, most people seem to want to wallow in it.

When people are miserable the brain send endorphins to ease the pain. Apparently people become addicted to these endorphins and sabotage themselves to keep generating them. These poor souls stumble from failure to failure not realizing they are creating a vicious circle that eventually leads to alcoholism, drug addiction and poverty.

As humans our default programming is ease and comfort. This is why we shy away from hard work and stressful situations. This is way why we too often say something can't be done when in reality we simply don't want to do it.

Also as humans we are hard wired to resist any challenge to our already accept beliefs. There are six obstacles to overcome those objections. Here's how people respond. 1) Resist 2) resist 3) resist, but with a clearer understanding of the new concept and how it might work. 4) Resist but with a willingness to give it a try. 5) Partial acceptance, upon discovery that the new concept does work. 6) Full acceptance and an enthusiasm to inform others.

So I'm rarely surprised when people tell me they think creating a positive mindset is a waste of time. I simply accept the fact that I have six obstacles to overcome and get right to work.

Here's another fact. When people attend seminars they are often impressed and leave determined to incorporate what they've learned into their daily lives. But although the intention is there, the application often falls short. This is because people forget much faster than they remember. And every time you learn something new, what you previously learned is pushed to the background.

This is why it's so important to write things down. When you learn something, write it down and review again and again until it become part of your daily routine. That's why I instructed you to watch the positive thinking videos over and over until it is a skill that you have mastered.

I must admit that I often fail in this regard. I do write these new lessons down, but in my eagerness to learn more I fail to review those notes and within a week or so I forget about them, rendering that new information useless.

So as you read this book, take notes and review them daily, if it's a new skill, perform it daily until it's easily done. When I was a kid I taught myself to play guitar. Became good enough to make money playing in a band.

My point is I haven't picked up a guitar in fifteen years yet if I did, not only would I know how to play it, within a few hours I would be as good as I was in my youth.

And that how you need to look at making money for retirement. If you study it and get good at it, the potential to make a lot of money is within your reach.

But only if you acquire a positive mindset. Without it the first few obstacles you encounter will likely cause you to lose faith and give up. What you need to understand is that each day more people are using the methods I outline in this book to make additional monthly passive income.

In addition to getting a positive mindset, you will need to get out of your comfort zone. This is also where a lot of people fail. I'll give you an example. When I was first marketing my books it was suggested that I create a Facebook ad, as

Facebook made it possible to laser-target my potential customers.

But I had never done that before and I hesitated. Tried to work around it. However when I discovered the influx of traffic my competition was getting with Facebook ads I knew I had to at least try it.

So I went to YouTube and typed in **How to Create a Facebook Ad.** There were several instructional videos so I picked one and followed it. Within an hour I had created my own Facebook ad. I now regret having waited so long.

So the take away is this: If you want money for retirement there will be several instances where you will need to step outside your comfort zone. You will be hesitant at first as I was but do it anyway. No life-threatening horror will befall you.

 Instead you will have acquired a new skill that can come in handy in matters other than making money for retirement.

And that's the next thing. Try to learn something new, or acquire a new skill or accomplish something each and every day and write it down. At the end of a month you will be amazed at all you have accomplished.

One last thing on preparation. **<u>NO EXCUSES</u>**. If you decide to go ahead, do not TRY, do not, GIVE IT A SHOT, do not, SEE HOW IT GOES. Those are all pre-excuses, created to soften the blow of failure.

Remember the positive mindset. You will succeed, you will accomplish your goals and you will not stop when you are tired, you will stop when you are done!

So Let's Get Started

It's best to dive right in. If you've decided to learn how to make additional money for retirement, then let's get right to it. Because serious people get things done. They think it over, weigh the pros and cons and make up their minds to either begin or move on to something else.

Those are the people who succeed. They are the ones who step outside their comfort zones and do things they are uncomfortable with. For example, because I'm in the publishing business it became necessary for me to occasionally speak before a large crowd of people. At the time I was very uncomfortable doing that. So I stopped and asked myself, *When I'm part of the crowd, what do I want from the speaker?* The answer was I wanted information that benefitted me.

It was that realization that changed my attitude. I wasn't on stage to try to get them to like me, I was there to provide the information they wanted. I was doing them a service. I was helping them. And personally I enjoy helping people.

Problem solved.

My point is there will be steps in this process that you have never attempted before and you will be hesitant about doing them. That's human nature. We're concerned about looking foolish, or screwing up. But keep in mind you're an experienced individual. You've looked foolish before, you attempted something and screwed it up.

BUT THAT"S HOW WE LEARN. We learn by **<u>DOING!</u>**

It's a sad fact but I've seen people with enormous potential fail because they just couldn't take the next step. They were afraid that if they added an opt-in box it would screw up their website. Or if they gave their social to Amazon to get paid a commission, they would have their identity stolen.

The reality there is always the possibility that if you make a change to your website, you could screw it up. If that happens make a note of what you did wrong and create another website, If a company like Amazon asks for your social security number just remember that **<u>ANY COMPANY, WHETHER BRICK AND MORTAR OR ONLINE, THAT PAYS YOU, MUST REPORT THAT PAYMENT TO THE IRS.</u>**

When you were first employed by your nine-to-five job, you had to fill out a form which included a box for your social security number. The IRS requires this for wage and tax reporting. Online businesses like amazon and others that pay you a commission are required to do this as well.

You can however, get and Employer Identification Number (EIN) from the IRS. Once done you can use that instead. As for me, I just type in my social. I first thoroughly check the company out and make sure they are an established, accredited firm but in cases of companies like Amazon or eBay you don't need to be concerned. I get commissions from dozens of companies and haven't had any problems.

Before we get started there are two very important tools that will help you with the process. The first is www.Google.com

If you don't know something, go to Google and type your question into the search box. For example: One of the main ways to make money for retirement is affiliate marketing.

But what if you don't know what affiliate marketing is? No problem, go to Google and type in *affiliate marketing*, If you want to know more, go to www.wikihow.com

The reason I point this out is because there are so many ways to earn additional income online that it would require a book the size of the Encyclopedia Britannica to properly address them all. Once you find a niche that shows real potential, the best place to learn more about it is to consult Google and Wikihow

Google also comes in very handy when you are considering purchasing a product that will help grow your online business. For example, say you've decided to get into the tropical fish niche, and come upon a site that offers a product that claims to provide you with everything you need to start up and run a successful tropical fish online business.

First step? Look up that product on Google and read the reviews. AND MAKE SURE THE REVIEWS AREN'T WRITTEN BY THE WEBSITE THAT IS SELLING THE PRODUCT. (Yeah, they can be pretty sneaky sometimes.)

If the reviews are positive then take the next step. However, pay close attention to comments about customer service. One of the problems with purchasing products online is that once the money is paid and the 30 day guarantee is up, they are on to the next product and ignore all requests for help.

The other tool you'll need is http://youtube.com Say you create a website that makes bird houses to customers specifications.

They require a bird house built in a certain design you're not familiar with. In that case go to http://youtube.com or www.wikihow.com and type in the name of that bird house design and very likely there will be a video that shows you exactly how to do it.

Remember in this day and age there is nothing you cannot learn. In fact I have a website devoted to just that. It's called http://theundergroundcollege.com and it provides online courses for people looking to learn new skills or increase their knowledge to better improve their value in the job market.

That being said here is the first thing you need to do.

Create a new email address for your business.

Do not use your personal email address because once you get started you'll need to check your business email a few times a day. Keep it simple. Something like bobsbiz9@gmail.com or mikesco@aol.com If for some reason it gets spammed simply scroll to the bottom and unsubscribe. This doesn't happen much anymore because of recent government regulations. I personally haven't encountered spamming in over

2 years. But when you're new it's always a good to be cautious.

Over time your business email address will become your internet identity. As you improve your skills you'll want to learn who else is doing what you're doing and what success they are having. You may even want to partner with them. The point being, don't get the two entwined. Personal is personal and business is business.

Next I'm going to show you a number of ways people make money over the internet. But before I do I must point out that you can become overwhelmed by all the opportunities and spread yourself too thin. It's called *paralysis by analysis.*

People who succeed take the time to choose the niche and course of action that best fits them. Keep that in mind when you peruse the following options and websites. And should you find a money-making opportunity that you feel is a good fit, research that opportunity by going to Google and typing in that opportunity and add the word *review*. For example there are writers like myself who make money writing articles for corporations. I researched the best known of these companies and discovered that a number of writer reviews stated that company's uploading process was difficult and slow and suggested I use a different company that offered the same services and pay outs.

So do your due diligence. Remember that you're going into business and your competitors would rather you didn't succeed. Start small and easy and see how it goes. If you make $15.00 your first month, that's actually a good thing. It means you got the basics correct. You'd be surprised at the thousands of beginners who go charging after the big money offers without having made a single dime. Don't get dreamy-eyed at offers that promise big money fast! They only work for people who are very experienced in online marketing and understand the tiny nuances that dictate failure or success.

So start slow, get the feel for it and have some fun!

Now as for that $15.00 your first month, it is a gold mine. It means you've found something that works and makes you money. Want to make more? Just repeat what you did to make the first $15.00. As you get better at it, that $15.00 will turn into $45 a month, then $100 and so on.

When you decide to get started it is a good idea to create a PayPal account www.paypal.com Its free and its one of the best ways to ensure all transactions are on the up and up. They make sure no one gets paid until the product is delivered and the customer satisfied.

So here's a breakdown of many (but certainly not all) of the ways you can make money for retirement. I will start with simple processes that make little money but also require little effort. In all cases make sure you read the terms of service. Many sites will close your account if you try to create a duplicate to increase your commissions. So read the rules, obey them and you should be fine. One last note. I neither approve nor disapprove of these sites or their products. They are merely the most successful. Note* If you are reading this as a paperback or listening as an audiobook it's a good idea to write down the site's URL's for reference to type into your computer. For e books you only need click on the highlighted links URL

<u>Here are the most popular websites that provide money in return for a service of some sort.</u>

www.cashcrate.com With Cash Crate you can make money by trying new products, taking surveys, getting cash back on products you regularly buy and posting offers and ads on your website. It doesn't pay out much money but it points out many of the free opportunities available to make some easy cash.

www.ebates.com If you do any shopping online this is a must have. With ebates you get up to 25% off on purchases plus additional cash for referring someone to the program. This applies to just about everything you buy. Also check out www.mrrebates.com for similar cashback opportunities.

www.dollarsurveys.net As simple as it can get. Enter you PayPal email address, take a quick survey and get paid. It's not much but you are getting paid simply by giving your opinion. Others that offer payment for taking surveys are www.globaltestmarket.com www.mysurvey.com www.clearvoicesurveys.com

You can also make money by writing reviews for various company's products and services

www.socialspark.com http://payforpost.com

At www.expotv.com you get paid by giving a video review of products you like and own.

www.writedge.com This site pays you to write articles and bookmark websites. Other popular money producing sites in this genre are

www.hubpages.com www.infobarrel.com
www.shetoldme.com www.bestreviewer.com

At http://sponsoredtweets.com You get paid to
tweet, blog, take photos and videos.

Here are a number of sites that pay you to do freelance work.

www.elance.com If you are an experienced
professional in any online genre, Elance can
provide you with real money making opportunities

www.iwriter.com If you can write well and
like research, you can make a bit of money here.

www.fiverr.com This is the grandaddy of all
online service providers. A friend of mine started a
now lucrative business by offering his professional
editing services for one dollar a page. Now
independent, he charges $3.00 per page and has a
long list of clients.

Are you an artist, photographer or musician?

You can make money selling your photos,
illustrations and music on such sites as
www.Istockphoto.com www.shutterstock.com
www.fotolia.com

Make money teaching others what you do

As mentioned earlier I have a website that provides video tutorials that teaches students varies skills and trades. Say for example, you are a professional car transmission specialist. You could create a video showing how to repair various transmissions on several types of cars. Or you are a highly experienced woodworker, you can do a video showing how to do intricate type of woodworking (You've no doubt seen the home improvement show Ask this Old House). In fact, you can make money with almost any form of specialty. Teach chess, how to play the banjo, woodworking, organic farming, you name it. And you can charge whatever you want. To learn more go to udemy.com/

There are also way to make a good deal of money by writing a how to articles and charging $7-$10 dollars for it. Say you're a professional poker player. Write a five to six page article explaining the tricks of the trade, what to look for, what the odds are on certain hands etc. To learn more about this go to www.warriorforum.com

An important point to remember is that people who become rich are people who see a need and fill it. Do you know something people want to know? Then sell that information over the internet.

What it all boils down to is this. You find a niche. This is a product or service that you would be interested in selling, (how this is done will be discussed later.) Then you create a Landing page, which will also be discussed later. Then this landing pages gets you customers and these customers buy your product or services.

Just like having a brick and mortar store. The only difference is that you don't have to mortgage your house or take out a huge loan to get started.

Now let's talk about pay per click (PPC) advertising. This is where most online money is made.

This can be very lucrative but not something I'd advise when you're just starting out. It's better to be more experienced because other than www.Google.com/adsense YOU are paying every time someone clicks on your ad.

Here's how Google's AdSense works. You create a simple website and join the AdSense ad program. They scan your website to see who would be interested in visiting, then place ads on it that would be of interest to them. Every time someone clicks on that ad, you get a commission.

I must point out that it usually isn't very much but remember AdSense doesn't cost you a penny and its additional income that's generated without you doing a thing. Special note* NEVER CLICK ON A ADSENSE AD ON YOUR OWN SITE. DO NOT OFFER INCENTIVES FOR CLICKING ON AN AD. These are violations of Google policy and will get you permanently banned!

The other pay per click Google offers is Google/AdWords. This is where YOU pay a certain amount every time someone clicks on your ad. Again this is something I don't suggest you attempt early on because mistakes can wind up costing you a good piece of change. It will however be discussed at length later on.

Another very successful form of advertising is Facebook ads. The process of creating an ad is very simple and they walk you through it. In addition, you can laser target your ad to be seen by your intended buyer. Say for example you sell rare coins on your website. You can target your ads only to appear before people interested in rare coins. This way you're not spending advertising money on people who aren't potential prospects.

The reason I mention forms of advertising that I don't suggest you use until you become more experienced is the marketers offering money making programs know exactly how to target you.

They have years of experience knowing what buttons to push and how to close a sale.

This is not a bad thing, basically it's what marketing is all about. But I'm teaching you how to *make* money for retirement not how to *spend* money learning how. At least not until you have a good idea of what you're doing.

That being said I'm going to show you some other forms of advertising that produce excellent results but only for those who know how to use them.

We'll start with Pay-Per-View (PPV). You join a PPV group and they place your ad on targeted websites that cater to the clientele you want to market to. These groups often require a down payment that will be used to better market your ad. The more popular are www.leadimpact.com (Have a look at their "How it works tutorial" on their toolbar) and www.trafficvance.com

Then there is Cost-Per-Action (CPA) This is perhaps the best and the easiest way to make money but it's often difficult to become a member. Here's how it works. You find something people are interested in that has little competition. This is called a niche. Some of the most popular (and highly competitive) niches are weight loss products, dog grooming, exercise videos and

mortgage refinancing) then you go to
www.offervault.com and in the search box type in
the niche product. Offervault then provides a
listing of all the products available for you to
advertise on your website. You find something you
like and want to use it, BUT remember you must
first get the approval of the product owner.

If you're new, in many cases you will be
turned down because you have no proven record of
successfully selling anything online. For example I
was turned down by www.neverblue.com but
accepted by www.maxbounty.com but the place to
get started is www.offervault.com check out their
videos and tutorials. They are very helpful and will
give you a strong overall view on how to make
some real money without much effort. And keep in
mind these ads are proven sellers because they
have been tested repeatedly to ensure the seller
makes back their investment on the product or
service

Another way to make money is to sell your
own products on sites like Amazon and eBay. For
example, my company manufactures books and
video tutorials and ships them to Amazon to sell
on their site. When they sell, I receive the agreed
upon price and they keep a small fee. There is a
real advantage to selling on sites like Amazon and
eBay is because they have considerably more

traffic and gives the buyer the opportunity to give a review and return it if they are in some way dissatisfied with the product. You should note that Amazon charges a storage fee each year so if it doesn't sell you will have to pay for its return or pony up for another years storage.

On a personal note I have been very satisfied with Amazon.com They are very professional, very straight forward, pay commissions and sales on time and make their company's policies clear. You probably won't get rich marketing Amazon products on your website but I seriously doubt that you will ever be underpaid or cheated out of a commission.

Did you know you can actually sell products you don't own?

When I mention that I sell a gun that fires salt at high speed that kills flies, they ask how did I come up with the idea and where do I manufacture it.

Actually I do none of that. A friend told me about the salt gun and I just had to see it in action. So I went on YouTube and typed in **salt gun kills flies** and watched the video.

I loved it! So I went to Amazon to see if they had it. They did, so I immediately scrolled down to the bottom of the page, clicked on the link that read **Become an Affilaite** and followed the instructions. Once accepted into the program, I went back to the bug-a-salt page, scrolled down to the ASIN number copied it then went back to the affiliate page and pasted it on the get link box. Once entered I got the code and pasted it on my website www.czarscoolstuff.blogspot.com

I need to point out that there is a process to inserting products links into a website which I will explain later. Right now I want to stress the opportunities not the mechanics.

As mentioned earlier, Amazon is a good company to partner with but they don't pay the highest commissions. If you're looking for companies that pay commissions in the 35%-75% range then start looking into www.cj.com and www.clickbank.com CJ is mega big with products from almost everywhere but they are only interested in sites that perform. If you're new, then hold off joining until you have a popular website with a good amount of traffic.

Clickbank is the better choice for newcomers. Simply go to their site and click on **marketplace** on the top toolbar. Once there you will see on the left a column of red boxes in numerous categories. These are the affiliate offers. What you do next is click on the category that best fits your chosen niche. For example, mine is e-business and e-marketing. When I click on that I'm taken to the results page.

At the time of this writing the top product is Google Sniper. The average sale nets you $151.98. If you click on the products headline you will see their sales page where they promote the product. It's a video that shows you how Google Sniper can make you lots of money.

Guess what, that video and others like it are actually sales pages. And as such they are all going to tell you how wonderful their product is and why you should sell it on your website. But how good is it really?

Well I'm going to teach you a trick to find out. Clickbank has an alternate website called www.cbengine.com Once there you will see on the top left, **the top selling products** at the present time. However on the lower right you will see the **Find Products** box.

In the **top category** box chose your products category (again mine is e-business and e-marketing) then in the KEYWORD box type in the name of your product. I typed in Google Sniper and was taken to the www.cbengine site that is a little different than the regular clickbank site.

For example, if you scroll down for more details you will see a gravity icon. Click on that, then scroll down and you will see a graph showing how the product has been selling since it was introduced. Google Sniper has had consistent sales for 2 years now so if that's your niche it would be a good product to offer on your site.

On the other hand if sales are fading, it's likely the product has outlived its usefulness and probably won't make you any money.

So once you've found a product you feel will perform well for you, go back to the clickbank website and click on the promote code on the right of the offer. It will provide you with an affiliate link that includes your clickbank ID. Before getting started, read the clickbank terms of service regarding payouts and commissions. I know people who had their commissions pushed back because they didn't follow the payout directions.

Again, how to insert affiliate links into your website will be discussed later in the book.

I could make this entire book about various ways to make money online but that might do more harm than good. Every successful person who has created numerous online income streams first created a clear strategy on how they would proceed. They did not sample this and try that.

They found a niche that they were interested in, devoted themselves to learning all they could about it and set out to build their business.

The last online opportunity to consider is a company called www.buildit.sitesell.com It is perhaps the most highly respected affiliate program on the market today. What SBI site sell does is teach you exactly how to make your online business a success. They have programs that evaluate your niches and marketing plans and present you with a clear outline of what you will need to do to make a steady income. It is a carefully worked out video program that you can watch whenever you want and learn at your own pace.

I personally was a member for 6 months and I can say from my own experience that you'll find no better teaching program than the one they offer.

It costs only $30 a month AND if within 90 days you decide it's not for you, they refund your payments, no questions asked. This is the only company that I would personally recommend. However, I think it best if you first try out some of the options presented in this book before committing. I say this because you first need to get a basic knowledge of making money in this manner and build some confidence in your ability to do so.

Once you start seeing that it works and want to take a step to the next level then decide whether or not you want to sign up with SBI Site Sell.

Building Your Online Business

The next step is to find out what people are looking to buy. When you get right down to it, that's the only thing you need to know to make additional money for retirement. The reality is that everybody is looking for something. Your job is to find it and sell it to them. For example, you're looking for ways to make more money for retirement, so are a lot of middle-aged men and since I knew exactly how to do just that, I wrote this book… which you bought.

Here's how you get started. Sit down and make a list of tasks that you enjoy doing. Leave that list open and in an area where you spend a lot of time. Like the end table of your easy chair. Make the list as large as you can, spend a couple of days doing it.

Why? Because you are creating possible niche markets that can make you quite a bit of money when properly established. For example: As a writer and publisher some of the services my company offers http://aripublishing.com is ghost writing, editing, how to create a book, how to get a book published and how to market a product. A friend of mine knows HTML coding and has a site that offers his services. Another has exceptional organizational skills and her website offers her services to people who need their homes and offices reconfigured to their maximum efficiency.

Another is an accomplished salesman and his website offers his services to businesses that need to find customers. Another has a website that writes personal thank you, birthday, condolence, and anniversary cards for busy professionals. Another has a website that sells a video tutorial on how to use the Evernote program. Another's website sells a very popular video that prepares freshmen college students on what to expect, what opportunities to take advantage off and a very popular addition that explains what actions to take should their car breakdown while on route to or from home.

So the question is, how did I find out that there was a large market looking for this product? The answer is I researched it on Google's Keyword Planner, which is a free program that you can access once you sign up for Google's AdWords program. For set up instructions go to www.youtube.com and type in the search box, *how to set up Google's Keyword Planner*. There are several videos on this so view the most recent because Google changes its set up every few months.

To be successful you will need to use this product on a regular basis. Why? Because it provides the keywords that drive traffic to your website. Another helpful site is www.keywordtool.io

Here's a word of warning. Almost everyone making additional income online uses Google's Keyword Planner. Google doesn't like people using their software programs without paying. As of the time of this writing is appears that Google intends to make you create an AdWords ad before allowing access to their Keyword Planner. You can bid as little as $5.00 and kill the ad when the $5.00 is used up. Once you actually create an ad you will have access to the Keyword Planner whenever you like.

Here's an option. Go to www.longtailpro.com and sign up for their free ten day trial. It contains a very effective tutorial and contains some useful additions that the Keyword Planner does not. For example: Once you find the right keyword to use in your website URL address, this product lets you know right away if that domain name is available for purchase.

Which brings us to creating a website. To access the Keyword Planner you will have to set up an AdWords account and one of the first questions it asks is what is your website URL. Since you are likely not experienced enough to set up a fully functional WordPress website yet, it's best to create a disposable free website that will give you access to the Keyword Planner, without having to have a professional website created.

5 years ago I created a free site and that website is still widely read. The link is http://zackaryrichards.blogspot.com I don't really sell anything on that site because Google owns it and as such can shut it down at any time.

To create a blogger website go to http://blogger.com and follow the simple cut and paste directions. Keep it simple and don't reveal any personal information you wouldn't want shared.

So what exactly are keywords?

Keywords are the words or phrases people type into Google's search box when they want information on something. Say I want to buy the Beatles Anthology box set. To find out where to get it I would type *Beatles anthology box set* into the search box and Google would provide me with a list of where to get it.

The keyword here is *Beatles Anthology Box Set*.

Here is where the keyword planner comes in. Once you open Google's Keyword Planner click on the top box that reads **Search for a new keyword using a phrase website or category.**

Type Beatles Anthology Box in that box, then scroll down to the blue box that says **Get Ideas** and click on it.

Then click on the box that reads **Keyword Ideas**

What you will see is a list of keywords, the amount of times per month people are typing in those exact words and the rate of competition you will have should you use that keyword in your website.

So let's say you have a website called bobsmusicreviews.com and you write a review of the Beatles Anthology titled *Bobs Music Reviews/Beatles Anthology Box Set.* And on that review you have an affiliate link where, should they click on it and buy the box set, you get a commission from that purchase.

That's great in theory but lousy in practice. Why? Because there are already ads for that product on Google's first page and from Amazon and other heavy hitters that you won't be able to outrank in the standings, meaning your website offer will be buried on page one hundred and something.

What you want to do is find something that people want but only a few people are selling. You see, it's no different than having a regular brick and mortar business is it? But the question is, how do you find these people and the products or services they are they looking for?

If you're listening to this as an audio book you're going to need to pause and get a pen and paper because I'm going to explain exactly how to find what people are looking to buy, how much you can make selling to them, where you can get the product and how much competition you will be facing.

Ready?

Go to Google Keyword Planner and start typing in trigger keywords. Trigger keyword don't have an exact product, they are words that people type in BEFORE or AFTER the product or service itself. Here are some examples of trigger keywords:

How to, learn to, find, broken, build, where, calculate, directory, during, effect, enhance, cost, answers, basics, beginner, Want to know, diagram, guide, guides, maps, help, hints, leak, lessons, tutorial, lower. You get the hint.

So for example you go to your Keyword Planner and type in *lower*

You'll note that the vast majority of associated keywords have high number of searches but low competition. Take the keyword example of *lower back exercise.* There is 1900 Google searches every month with low competition.

Seems pretty good so far. But there's a lot more to it. For example, let's look up the competition on Google. When I type in the phrase *lower back exercise* I see there are 170,000 results. But there aren't any advertisements. Advertisements are usually situated on the top and bottom of the list and as a right column. Since there aren't any there (as of the time of this writing) it means I can get that keyword for about 12 cents a click.

Not bad but first let's check Google trends. So we go to http://Google.com/trends and in the search Google trends box I type *lower back exercise* and discover that interest in that topic has been steadily increasing over the last few years.

So far, so good.

Now go to www.keywordspy.com and see what the competition is. At the time of this writing there is no competition.

Next step is to check www.clickbank.com and www.offervault.com and see what kind of affiliate programs are available. Under back pain, which is really what people are looking for when they type in lower back exercise, Clickbank has an offer that pays nearly $50 a sale and Offervault has one that pays $18 just for a lead. (Meaning they don't have to buy anything, they just input their name and email address)

Not bad. Now let's look at domain names

Go to http://hostgator.com then to the above toolbar and click on domains. When the search box appears type in the name that closely fits your offer. For example at the time of this writing lowerbackexercise.net is available with 1,900 searches a month with low competition for that exact term and no ads on the front page.

Looks real good. BUT! Keep in mind these things change daily so it's very unlikely that this keyword and domain will be such a good find by the time you read this so don't copy, instead use the trigger word method I just showed you.

Another point to keep in mind is that like any business, you're going to try a certain keyword or keyword phrase that you think is going to make you a ton of money. That is until you follow the directives I just showed you and discover two thirds of the way through that you got a dud on your hands.

This happens to us all so don't get discouraged. 7 out of 10 businesses fail. The advantage you have is that you didn't have to take out a loan or mortgage the house only to discover that you made a rookie mistake somewhere along the way.

The more you do it the better you'll get. And once you get that first big hit, you'll be sold. And why wouldn't you be? You spent about an hour setting up a website or outsourced its creation and now it's making you money every month without you lifting a finger.

I suggest you start with the easy things mentioned in the previous Let's Get Started chapter. Surveys, product reviews, coupons, ad placements etc. True they won't make you much money but it will help you understand how the process works. Just like you, everyone is trying to find out what people want and how much they are willing to pay for it, so they can find that product and sell it to them.

Now I understand that we middle-aged folk are short on patience, which means that you're not going to be satisfied making just a few dollars a day but there is a method to this madness.

Let me tell you a quick story. A home improvement salesman makes the biggest sale of his career selling lumber to a new housing complex. The commission on the sale will be by far the highest he ever received. He struts into his bosses office with the signed order in hand, hands it to him and with a big smile on his face asks his boss, "So what do you think of that?"

"Very, very, impressive," the boss replies. "This sale of lumber is the largest we have ever sold to a customer. Great job! Just one question," he added looking the work order over. How many boxes of nails did he order?"

The salesman's smile disappeared.

This is an important point. Although your goal is to find out what people want and sell it to them, it is also important to take a moment to ask yourself, what else might they need?

Returning for a moment to the lower back exercise website. What is a person typing in lower back exercise really looking for? Odds are he /she has lower back trouble, lower back pain, maybe arthritis, sciatica, fibromyalgia, a magnesium deficiency or a number of other back related ailments.

Does your site address these possibilities and offer solutions? If not, why not? They are at your site and need help. Make sure all the help they need is available.

So how do you find out what they need? Let's start with www.Google.com Go to Google.com and in the search box type in **resell rights.** Then scroll down until you see **Master-resale-rights.com** Click on that link. Then in the search box type *lower back exercise*. Scroll down until you see **20 articles on lower back pain**. Click on it and you'll see that you can purchase all twenty articles for $1.69 and well as all the rights to them. Meaning you can change them and add affiliate offer links inside the articles. *(NOTE* If an article contains medical information don't touch that unless you are a certified medical professional. Otherwise the changes I'm suggesting is something like adding an affiliate link to a vitamin company for example: Back pain is often cause by vitamin deficiencies so click this link to get a free bottle of the best vitamin for middle-aged men Centrum Silver.)*

Also it is important that you rewrite the article using your own words. The reason is these articles have likely been sold before and someone may already have them on their website so rewrite them so Google won't punish you for using duplicate content.

As for your website, you can feature three of those rewritten articles on separate pages. Then at the end of each article, ask if they would like to know more on how to get rid of back pain, if so, click here. They click on a link which takes them to an opt-in box where they type in their name and email address. In return for that information they receive the 17 remaining articles which you don't need to rewrite because you're not posting them online.

Plus you now have their email address so when a new offer arrives at Clickbank or Offervault that addresses their concerns, you can email them and advise them of that new offer. An opt-in box is essential to your website. It collects the names and email addresses of your potential customers. How to get one and set it up on your site will be discussed later.

The Importance of a LEAD MAGNET

A lead magnet is an offer that your perspective customer will find engaging enough to be willing to give you their name and email address in exchange for it. You've no doubt seen them yourselves. "Get a free subscription to... 10 ways to lose 30 pounds in thirty days... new miracle cream makes age spots vanish overnight...

<u>One of the best ways to get customers is to offer them something for free</u>. People love free. And they will love you if the thing you send them for free is actually something they can use.

Going back to the lower back exercise website, the resell rights you purchased for $1.69 is now creating 7 new customer leads a day. Plus several have written to say that the peanut oil method outline in article 7 has done wonders for their back pain.

These are known as testimonials. People LOVE testimonials because nobody wants to be the first to try anything. But if someone already tried it and liked it, and it did for them what it claimed it could do... Well you likely got a future sale and possibly another testimonial.

But I'm getting ahead of myself. Putting together a successful income stream is like putting together a car piece by piece. You may not understand why it's being built a certain way but when you finish and start it up, it will all become clear.

So it this point I'm going to assume that you have dabbled with the surveys and such and would like to know exactly what is entailed when it comes to creating a an actual business website.

So here goes.

You start with Google keyword Planner and start typing in the trigger keywords. This will take a bit of time and research but no more than a few hours. When you find one that passes all the tests, buy the domain name. Go to www.hostgator.com go to the toolbar and click on domains in the search box. Try to get a .com because that's what most people assume a domain name ends with but .net and .org and .info are also acceptable if .com is not available, as in the case of our earlier www.lowerbackexercise.net if you can't get any on those three, try a different domain name.

The next item you will need is a web hosting account. You have a website name but you need to have it placed on the internet. There are several available but www.hostgator.com is the most popular, it only costs one cent for the first month plus you won't have to do a domain DNS switch because both the domain name and the webhosting are handled by the same company. Once at their site, sign up for their baby plan. It provides you with unlimited hosting so you can keep creating new domains without having to pay for their hosting. You will likely want to switch things around as you become more proficient, but for now simple is best.

The next step is to set up a Word Press website.

Word of advice. Yes you may want to continue with the free website you created since you didn't have to pay for a domain name or webhosting. But the serious pitfall with those free sites is that YOU DON"T OWN THEM. The company that supplied you with them DOES and at any time they, without your knowledge or permission, can take that website down. They are also highly restrictive when it comes to optimizing your website to improve your sales and increase your ranking on Google. Blogger, for example, is owned by Google and they do not allow search engine optimization (SEO) of any kind. That being the case marketwise, you are considerably hobbled, especially since search engine optimization is critical if you want to get that all important spot on the first page of a Google search.

So to start go to www.youtube.com and type in **how to set up a WordPress website**. There are quite a few there and you should have no trouble following them. Note* try to locate the most recent video because WordPress is constantly updating their site to keep hackers and spammers and other creeps out.

If you find setting up a WordPress website too complex for you at this early stage then go to http://fiverr.com Fiverr will quickly become one of your best buddies. I use it all the time to do tasks I'm not proficient in or simply don't have the time to do. All you need to do once you're on the fiverr.com site is to go to the toolbar, click on Programming and Tech and then click on Word Press. There for $5.00 you can hire someone to set up your website for you.

After you get it back and approve it, be sure to change your site's password. Not that I anticipate any problems, it's just that you don't want anyone other than yourself to have access to your site.

Fiverr is also great for a number of things. You can order a spokesperson presentation that explains your website and the products or services it provides. I have one on my http://aripublishing.com site. You can hire these people to optimize your website, add links and handle social networking and much, much more.

For best results view the number of gigs they have already completed and the testimonials they received from their customers. It is also good to check and see how long it will take for the job to be completed. Once you get started creating your online income stream you won't want to be slowed down waiting for a certain task to be completed. Here's another important piece of information regarding fiverr. Always remember that you can reject the finished product if you are dissatisfied. It doesn't usually happen if you check their credentials first but sometimes you can get a slipshod job. If this happens simply cancel the order and find somebody else.

It's too early in the game to get into the marketing complexities. I just wanted to reassure you that some of the complex hurdles you may encounter with your online business can often be easily handled with a 5 dollar gig on fiverr.

When creating your webpage remember that simple is best. Years of market research has shown that sites with complex designs and colors distract rather than attract.

Another important fact to remember when you start your online business is that PEOPLE ARE ONLY INTERESTED IN WHAT BENEFITS THEM. In my book *The Best Book on How to*

Sell Anything Online I go into detail regarding the proper way to create a compelling headline, sales page and opt-in.

For example: Many professionals make the mistake of opening their website by introducing themselves, what they do, how long they've been doing it and where their business is located.

What they don't realize is that **people don't care**. So you need to grab their attention first! Here are a few Headline examples. In the organic gardening genre:

Create a flourishing, pest-free, chemical free, organic garden guaranteed to produce the biggest and healthiest fruits and vegetables with my FREE organic gardening guide.

For breast augmentation:

Are you disappointed with your breasts? I can make you love them again!

For weight loss:

Would you like to Learn Three Simple Steps that will cause you to

lose up to 30 pounds in as little as 90 days, guaranteed?

Did you notice how those headlines immediately grabbed your attention? Take for example the title of this book. *Money for Retirement-The Middle-Aged Man's Survival Guide.* **Money for Retirement**-is anyone NOT interested in that topic? Subtitle: **The Middle-Aged Man's Survival Guide**. If you're a middle-aged man like myself then you are particularly interested in bolstering your retirement income. The point is I have laser-targeted my potential customers.

That's basically all the information you need to get started. But before we move on to the next chapter it's important that we review the steps that brought us here and make sure the process of increasing your retirement income is understood and ready to be applied.

Number 1 You have created a business email address and have verified that it works.

Number 2 You have visited the websites mentioned earlier in this book. Perhaps made a few bucks doing surveys and product reviews

Number 3 You have familiarized yourself with both Google, Wikihow and YouTube and understand how to use them.

Number 4 You have created a FREE PayPal account for online business transactions.

Number 5 You have created a FREE website on Blogger (Wix also offers free websites) Choose whatever you feel more comfortable with.

Number 6 You've visited http://fiverr.com and looked around to see what products or services could best benefit your business.

Number 7 You have gained access to the Google Keyword Planner by either setting it up yourself or hiring someone from fiverr.com to do it. Access to Keyword Planner is an absolute necessity.

Number 8 You have added Google AdWords to your website and are featuring ads revealent to your websites niche.

Number 9 You have tried a few of the trigger words to find out what products or services people are searching for.

How to Make a Passive Income with Little Effort

It's probably best if you read through the entire book before setting out to find your niche market. The reason for this is at this stage of your life you don't need difficult and trying. You've likely had your share of that and now want to do somethings that's fun and adds to your monthly income.

For example, I write and publish books. I love doing it and the more books I write the more money I make. I have a friend who created a medical coding website for medical professionals. His site takes the complex process of medical compliance with government regulations and simplifies it. Having done just that for decades working for hospitals he now makes a very lucrative income selling his medical coding tutorials.

In addition, he has received several offers to purchase his website, but he won't sell because he loves researching and improving the technology. It's what gets him up in the morning and entertains him throughout the day.

I would like whatever niche you decide on to do the same for you.

Because there are so many ways to make money online there are various schools of thought as to which is the most lucrative. Actually the two main ones work quite well. The first method is to create small simple sites using trigger keywords, filling them with ads and offers and advertising them on Google AdWords and Facebook. It works if you've done your website setup as explained in the previous Building Your Business chapter.

The second is creating an authority site. This is often more difficult to do. The reason is competition. In order to make money with an authority site you need to become the "Go To" site people bookmark and visit often.

This also requires learning search engine optimization. (SEO) The popularity of your site depends on a number of factors such as the number of other authority sites that are linked to yours. For example, say you had a fishing and camping site. It would benefit your site greatly to have a link to it from such mainstays as www.wildlife.org or the Wildlife Conservation Society www.wcs.org or the national wildlife federation www.fws.org

I don't suggest you go the authority site method at this early stage. It take a while to become proficient and it's geared toward those looking to make really big money with really big and powerful sites. And unless you have years of experience you're not ready for that yet.

Now let's talk about competition. It is essential that you know what the competition is before setting up a website and trying to make money with it. Too often beginners create a website that simply has too much competition and no matter what they do they will not be able to get anywhere near the front page of Google. For example, if you are considering weight loss sites, fitness sites, dog grooming or training or how to make money sites you're going to find the competition very stiff. However, you can get a piece of those niches if you specialize in certain aspect of it. It requires a lot of keyword research and ad testing but it can be done.

I feel the best way to start out is the simple site method. It's simple and easy and although it doesn't generate that much income at first as you improve your skills, you will likely improve your monthly income.

So ask yourself this question. How much additional income would you be happy with? An extra $1,000 a month? $2,000? $5,000? How much work would you be willing to put in to attain that goal?

First let's look at what you need to accomplish regarding income. To generate $1,000 a month you would need to generate $33.33 per day in profit. For $2,000, $66.66 a day for $5,000 you would need $166.66 per day. Note that $2,000 a month equals and additional $24,000 a year in additional income.

And the best part is you don't have to leave your house to earn it.

Once you decide that you are going to set up an online business, here are the things you are going to need to be successful. And before I list them let me point out that you don't want to be an innovator when just starting out. Too often newcomers fail because they see what's required and decide to skip that part or not get that software or use a free site to sell their product or service and then wonder why they aren't making any money. Use the tried and true simple method when starting out. The goal is to see how quickly you can start generating some income. At first it doesn't matter how much, it only matters that you are making more money than you are spending to make it. Once you are successful, all you need do to make more money is do more of what you did.

So here's what you'll need:

1. **You'll need to purchase a domain name.** Go to www.hostgator.com click on domains and see if the one you want is available. A domain name will cost you about 12 dollars a year. Purchase one that is as close a fit to what you are selling as possible. For example we used the trigger words to find lower back exercise, researched it and bought www.lowerbackexercise.net

2. **You will need to purchase webhosting.** This will cost you about 8 dollars a month for hosting as many sites as you want. There are several places where you can buy this but when starting out stick with www.hostgator.com Buy their baby plan so you can create all the websites you want without paying for additional hosting.

3. **You will need a WordPress website.** Once you purchase a domain name and webhosting you can create a WordPress website using hostgators Quickinstall program. They will walk you through the entire process. Now write this down. **IT WILL TAKE BETWEEN 24-48 HOURS BEFORE YOUR WEBSITE WILL BECOME ACTIVE.** So many newcomers forget this and panic once they set up their site and discover that they can't access it.

You will receive an email from hostgator when your site becomes active and you can begin to build it. Research other sites in your niche and see how their websites look, especially the ones that are on Google's first page and imitate them. Remember you are not here to innovate, you are here to sell. Don't try to reinvent the wheel, do what has been proven to work.

4. **You will need an auto responder.** Not at first but once you have collected more than 10 email addresses to get your free offer it will become a necessity as your email provider won't let you send emails to more than ten addresses at a time. An auto responder can send to as many email addresses as you want. It is also the place where you get your opt-in box. An opt-in box is where people type in their name and email address to get the FREE offer/Lead Magnet. The one we offered in our www.lowerbackexercise.net site was for the Free articles on back pain. There are three places where you can get an opt-in box. I use www.aweber.com it costs 19.00 dollars a month. www.mailchimp.com is free at first so you might want to go with them until you become more experienced. There are several videos on YouTube on how to set it up, or

you can just have it done by someone on fiverr and save yourself the trouble.

5. <u>You will need a landing page</u> This is essential. When you advertise on places like Google or Facebook you'll need a place where, once your ad is clicked on, you potential customer can see all you have to offer AND click on the link that takes them to your opt-in box. In my opinion the best site to get your landing page is <u>www.instabuilder 2.0</u> First of all you only pay a one-time fee. Most of the others charge monthly. Plus it has a complete set of video tutorials that will walk you through the set up process (just click on HELP on the toolbar) as well as how to maximize your landing page to attract the most potential buyers and it is free for the first 60 days!

6. <u>You will need to install Plug-ins</u> These add-ons make it possible for your site to be seen by more people. Opinions vary on the type and number you need to install (the great majority are free) but the two must haves are the Google XML site map and SEO by Yoast. The XML site map is so Google can find your site and index it and SEO by Yoast to optimize your site.

7. <u>You will need traffic.</u> In order to sell something you will need customers. That's a given. There are two ways to get traffic. One is to advertise to get traffic (this is called organic traffic which we will discuss in a later chapter) or you can outright buy traffic from sites like www.buysellads.com or http://udimi.com/

8. <u>You will need to make sure your site is indexed with Google.</u> To make sure go to www.Google.com and in the search box type in site:yourdomainname.com (in our example it would look like this site:lowerbackexercise.net and click enter. If you website doesn't appear at the top or you can't access it. Neither can anyone else. So fix this problem before doing anything else with the site. Again its fiverr. com to the rescue.

A person whose emails I always open is Russell Brunson. Why? Because when I do, I almost always learn something that benefits me. And because I am on his list, I received two of his paperback books by simply paying the shipping. They are marketing textbooks that I refer to on a regular basis. They presently sell on

Amazon for over $20 each plus shipping. Here is some very valuable information I learned from him.

Fine-tuning the niche you want to work in and the customer you want to do business with.

So let's assume you've found the niche you want to work in by going through the list you created of the tasks you enjoy doing.

The next step is to find the customer you want to do business with. The types you want to eliminate are the time wasters and the lookie-loos. These people want all your free stuff but don't buy anything, so the goal is to tailor your website and ads to attract the serious buyer.

To do this fashion your website in a way that attracts people who already have a basic knowledge of what you're offering. For example, if you were in the rare coin niche your website could have the word *numismatic* in its URL. Most people in the rare coin collection niche know exactly what numismatic means, in addition that keyword has 14,000 searches a month with low competition and there aren't any ads on Google for that term.

The next step is where do you find these people? Are they on forums? Do they subscribe to an ezine or newsletter? Are they a member of an organization? For example, there is a website called the American Numismatic Association www.money.org and they are just chock filled with people interested in rare coins. In developing your business take some time to figure out where your ideal customer is spending his time. Once done you have access to hundreds if not thousands of people interested in what you have to offer.

So what do we offer to attract them? So now that you know where to find them, what do you offer to get them to type their email address in your opt-in box? One option is to go back to the resell rights offer websites and get a book or audio or video and offer that. Or you can have something written to your specifications by www.iwriter.com Using the rare coins niche as an example, instruct them to create an article that provides whatever information you think they would want on rare coins. To find that out, go to Google, type in rare coin forums, join one and find out what questions are most commonly asked, then instruct the iwriter to create an article answering those questions. For example, I'm creating a video on how to insert a retargeting code into a Facebook ad because a lot of people want to know how to do that and would gladly give me their email address for that information.

Okay, you have built a list of interested consumers. Now what?

Now you provide them with as much value as possible. When you find out something new or have a tutorial that will benefit your customer tell them about it or give it to them. **Don't always be selling something.** The best way to lose a customer is to only contact them when you have something to sell. Your goal now is to become their friend, the guy who, when he emails you, provides something that's beneficial.

This is very important because people doing business online receive a number of emails a day and most of them are routinely deleted. I know because I do this myself. I'll purchase some online product and from that day on he's emailing me with some other thing to sell.

That guy get unsubscribed and deleted fast.

On the other hand there are emails that I will always open and open enthusiastically. These are from people who have shown me how to do various tasks that have benefitted my business, created plug-ins and software that reduced my workload. Showed me websites that got me great deal on products I routinely needed and so much more.

If you want to be successful, that's the guy you need to be. Because when you are that guy, people trust you. And people buy high-end products from people they trust. And as Russell says *Its a lot easier to sell high-end products to people who trust you.*

Remember to talk to them directly and provide value whenever you can. If you're losing subscribers then you are doing something wrong and you need to address it immediately. Go back to the basics and find out where and why you lost their interest.

It is much, much easier to keep a customer than to get a new one. So if they have a problem, get in there and fix it, even if it means money out of your own pocket. One bad online review of you and your product can cost you thousands of new and existing business.

How to Find a Niche that Makes Money

Of all the things necessary to create a consistent income online, finding the niche that works for you is the most important. In addition, it is often the most difficult.

But it doesn't have to be.

Your start looking where people congregate. And what I mean by that is go to places where a lot of people go. For example: YouTube. What are the most popular YouTube videos? Search on Google then check them out. Do any of them show potential for selling a product?

I'll give you an example. If you go to you tube and type in *funny cat compilation* you will see the top video has 47 million views. If you type in *videos for cats* you will see a video with over 1 million views and all it features is a group of birds eating birdseed on the ground. AND THERE IS NO LINK TO A WEBSITE! Which means this video with over 1 million viewers, who love all things cats, has no links to the products or services people who love cats would be interested in.

So ask yourself this question. What if you were to do the same thing? Take out your video camera and film birds eating seed. Or white mice running around or another cat playing with a ball? Cat people LOVE videos that their cats watch and interact with.

So you create a website that features a video that cats interact with and on it feature cat toys, cat furniture, cat health supplies etc. Then create a Facebook business or fan page with the same title as your website. Then run a Facebook ad with the title *Cats Love This Video* and when you set up the ad, in the interest box, type in *cat lovers*. Remember that video featuring birds eating seed was watched by 1 million viewers. **Now say of that 1 million, only one percent clicked on one of your cat based affiliate offers, and say only half of them purchased one of your products from which you get an average commission of 8 dollars per sale.**

Here's the math. 1,000,000 X 1% =10,000 clicks on your ads.

½ of those who clicked bought a product= 5,000 purchases.

The average commission of those purchases is 8 dollars. $8.00 X 5,000 = $40,000

FORTY THOUSAND DOLLARS!

You're probably saying to yourself, "That can't be right." But it is. And here's why.

When large companies advertise their products on television, radio, print and internet, close to 90% of that advertising budget is wasted. Why? Because those advertisements go out to everyone and only a very small percentage of those exposed to those ads are potential customers. Let's use a cosmetic company as an example.

Right off the bat 50% of the people watching those TV ads are men, and they don't wear makeup. Another 30% are women who wear little to no makeup. Another 10% are women who only buy specific cosmetics from the competition. That leaves only 10% who are interested but that's no guarantee they will buy.

By creating a Facebook ad that is only shown to people who love cats which our research has shown us has a huge amount of potential viewers, we can reasonably assume that, after seeing their cat interact with the video, will find it so cute they'll want to reward their cat with some kind of gift.

Which is precisely what your website offers.

I'll say it again, **"Forty Thousand Dollars!!"**

But say you're unsure your ad will attract customers. No problem, you can create an ad for a budget as little as $10 dollars a day. I'm going to walk you through the creation of Facebook ads later on in the book. For now, I want to impress upon you that YES you can make a healthy amount of money for retirement with just an hour or so of research each day.

Now, it's important to point out that it's going to take a bit of practice, and the realization that many of your early sites will make little to no money. It is by split testing your ads that you will see which ones are generating more income than they cost. This way you can kill off the duds and pour more of your ad budget into the ads that produce.

And the process is very easy to understand. It works like this. If you spend one dollars on ads and each one of those ads make you two dollars, you're in business. If on the other hand you're spending 3 dollars for an ad and it's only making you 2 dollars. You need to rework that ad until it becomes profitable. If it doesn't after two or three tries, you've got a dud for whatever reason, and you need to find something else to promote.

There is an old saying when it comes to making money, and that saying is, **steal it if you can.**

Now I'm not talking about putting on a mask and holding up banks. What I'm saying is find a money making process that works and make it your own. There is enough money to be made for everyone. And there are hundreds of ways that work. So don't try inventing your own. I can almost guarantee that someone else has already tried it and discovered for some reason that it didn't work.

The next place to look for possible niches is Facebook LIKES. Here are the top 5 most LIKED

Muscle Cars

Rock Climbing

Lacrosse

Dogs

Pop Music

If you go to Facebook and type muscle cars in the search box you will see several muscle car websites with over 100,000 likes. The top one, **Muscle Horsepower** has over 2.1 million likes.

So how can you monetize that? First create a muscle car based website. Then go to YouTube and search for muscle car crashes. Then pick one that has a high number of clicks but doesn't have a link to a website. Which means it's only being shown on YouTube. Then you click on share, then embed, copy the code, go to your website, click on new page or post, whichever is your home page then on the top right click on text. Then paste the embed code on the page, click update and you're all set.

Next step is to get some muscle car product affiliate links and paste them in some content.

As mentioned earlier if you find a niche that will likely pay off big but you don't know enough about it to write a home page article, just go to either Fiverr.com or Iwriter.com and hire one of their guys to write it for you.

Then, create a Lead Magnet (meaning give them something for free in exchange for their email address) and see how well it builds subscribers to your site.

Next, create a Facebook ad that targets muscle car fans and see how well it converts. Start with only a couple of dollars a day. Keep in mind that if you sell just one product that makes you $15 dollars a day and you're only spending $10 to get that sale, you're making a profit AND gaining a subscriber.

Now that you know it works, slowly increase your ad budget for as long as it continues to make you a profit.

Easy peasy.

Now I understand that this will likely take you out of your comfort zone, I felt that way at first too. Especially when I first reached the point where I was spending $100 dollars a day on ads. For a while I was in a state of panic. *What if nobody buys? What if they want a refund? What if they are dissatisfied and write a bad review.*

But numbers don't lie. Unless you're selling a truly terrible product you won't have to refund any money and you will make sales that bring in more money than you're laying out. It's always a good Idea to purchase the product yourself first, just to make sure it's worth the money.

For example I only promote 3 products throughout this entire book. They are SBI, Instabuilder 2.0 and Camtasia studio. I have owned or presently own all three of those products and can vouch for their value to my business.

In fact, here's a better idea. Find an article on CBS, Huffington Post, Reuters, Associated press, etc with the most shares and likes. Copy and paste that article into your website. It's perfectly legal as long as you give the proper credit to the original website and article writer.

Okay. So let's go over what we've learned so far. And I apologize if I sound repetitious but I want to make sure you don't fall victim to paralysis by analysis. The reason so many fail is they don't set their sights on a specific goal. They look into this and try that and consider something else and wind up accomplishing nothing.

Don't be that guy.

So let's go over the basics one more time:

Other than working for an online business, (surveys, writing copy, testing products etc.) There are two ways to make money on line. The first is building a lot of simple sites featuring services and products that are presently selling well, that have a lot of interest and low competition. You start by using the trigger words mentioned earlier to research possible niches. We did this and found the keyword lower back exercise. Then we followed all the steps outlined, tested again and again and following our research, decided to make a website called http://lowerbackexercise.net.

Then we went to Google, typed in resell rights and found a list of articles on back pain for sale. We bought the articles and the rights, rewrote and placed three of them on separate pages on our site and at the end of each article offered addition beneficial information. All they had to do was email you to get it.

In addition we inserted affiliate links into the articles to related product from which we received a commission. We also joined Google's AdSense program and ads related to our domain topic are being featured on a daily basis. And finally downloaded the Google analytics program plug in, and used it to see how many visitors we were getting and where they were coming from. (If you don't know how to do this contact fiverr.com to have it done for you or look up how on www.wikihow.com

Please note that the information provided by Google Analytics is what will help you laser target your potential customers. It will tell you **Who** is visiting your page, **What** age they are, **When** they arrive **Where** they are coming from and **How** much time they spent on your site.

With this information you can point your ads directly at your potential buyers. Say your website features articles on surfing and surfing equipment.

Google Analytics tells you that the majority of the people visiting your website live on the Atlantic and Pacific coasts. They are overwhelmingly males between the ages of 18-35, the website is visited mostly between the hours of 6pm to midnight EST, and the page they spend the most time on is the one that features an article on how to custom design a surfboard.

So instead of scattershot advertising like that cosmetic company we mentioned earlier, we set up our ads so they are only shown to males between the ages of 18-35, who live in coastal cities, and only between the hours of 6-12

Then we check the ads on the custom design a surfboard page to see which ones are selling and which aren't. We kill the duds and replace them with ads similar to the ones that are generating income. Armed with the Google Analytics information you are now able to lower the amount you pay for ads as well as greatly increase sales by featuring only the ads that make you money.

By using this process you will also learn which websites are producing for you and which aren't. Optimize the duds as best you can but if they still don't make you any money, try to sell them at auction on Go Daddy, and if they don't sell, let them expire when renewal time comes.

I know that sounds like a lot to do, but once you actually start doing it you will see it's not as complex as it sounds. Pretty soon you will be able to build a simple website in an hour or two.

"Really?!!" You say astonished.

Yep, and it's not that big a deal, nor is it expensive. Look at it this way. All you're laying out is about 12 bucks for each website. And that's per year. Say if that website only makes you $15 dollars a month. Let's look at the math. 15 dollars a month times for 12 months equals $180 dollars. Profit is $168 dollars from a website that you haven't touched or even looked at since you created it.

Now say you created 10 websites that only generated $15 dollars a month. Same math applies, you make $1,800 in profit.

Now what if you actually took the time to optimize the website and place Facebook ads in the amount of 10 dollars a day to a laser targeted audience that has a strong interest in what your website features. Say that single website is now generating $20 dollars a day. Now your profit is 300 dollars a month and 3,600 dollars a year. Now what if you optimized all ten of those sites? Well that comes to 36,000 dollars a year in pure profit. All earned while sitting at home.

This is why the simple sites method generates reliable income. If one of your sites starts failing it is easily replaced. Whereas if you have an authority site, a Google smack down for over optimizing will put you out of business for a while.

Still an authority site can generate enormous income especially if you become the **_go-to_** site for whatever niche you're in. For example Alex Becker's www.source-wave.com site generated him 2 million dollars last year. He makes his money by showing people like you and me search engine optimization. In laymen's terms he shows people how to get their websites to the first page of Google. This knowledge is exceedingly beneficial when it comes to getting and charging clients to have their website ranked.

I'll give you an example. You go to Google and type in plastic surgeons in Middleton, Delaware. At the bottom of the first page you notice that it's no longer featuring plastic surgeons, but instead where to find plastic surgeons, medical schools, and other topics not directly targeted to plastic surgeons. So you click down a few pages and find a plastic surgeon who is very qualified but whose website is languishing on page eight. So you email his office and tell him for 250 dollars a month you will get his website on the first page of Google and that the first month is free.

So using the skills Becker teaches on source-wave.com you optimize the site and within 6 weeks it's on the first page. The doctor send you a check for $250.00 each month. Then you move on to the next city and do the same thing. And this doesn't apply only to plastic surgeons, it can be used on any discipline whose sales depends on easy access on Google. Here's a few examples.

Construction

Financial professionals

Architects

Commercial Real Estate

Plumbing

Carpeting

Landscaping

Industrial equipment

Even consider the field you are in now. The point is, if your business is on Google's first page, its being seen by tens of thousands each day and the people in those industries listed above would happily pay 2000-10000 dollars a month for that ranking. And that translates into sales, BIG sales.

Alex Becker has over 500,000 email addresses and that list grows every day. Here's why. He sells by the 80%-20% rule. This means 80% of his emails feature useful information to website owners without selling anything. I have learned so much from him that to show my appreciation I have bought several of his products even though I rarely use Search Engine Optimization. I also open all of his emails. And that's important. Because regardless of what you're selling, the most important part of any website venture is to offer those who open your emails something that is beneficial to them.

For example: While surfing the web you come across a free plug-in that automatically transfers videos that you make with your computer's webcam to your website. This is what I would do. I would create an email for everyone on my list and here's what it would say.

Hi, It's Zackary Richards from Ari Communications and I just found this remarkable FREE plug-in that transfers any video you make with your computers webcam directly to your website. I've created a little video of my own to show you how to set it up. Here's the link to the Free Plug- in and the how to video LINK.

Enjoy!

Zackary Richards Ari Communications.

So what was accomplished here? Well, we've contacted our list and GAVE them something that may benefit them. We didn't sell anything. We didn't pitch anything. Just free benefits to show our appreciation of their being on our list. Now if you do this 8 out of ten times your list is going to open every email you send.

And here's another important point. Even when you have something to sell remember the 80-20 rule. Give them 80% useful beneficial content and use the last 20% to pitch your product. Believe me, if you follow this rule, not only will you easily build a very large list very fast, you will also be able to sell high end products because you have established yourself as a person who is trustworthy.

Even though you're tired of listening to me tell you that to succeed you must take it one step at a time, I'm going to keep doing it anyway. Too often I have seen people get bug-eyed when they see all the opportunities to make money online. They try to do too much too fast and they fail because they haven't established themselves in the marketplace.

There are a lot of get rich quick schemes on the net and people get duped because the pitch seems so logical. They see the testimonials, and the money charts and the large commission payouts and they ask themselves, why are they working so hard for a miserable boss when all they need do is follow this guy's instant money making plan and within 30 days they'll be financially independent and won't need that job? "Yessiree, that's what I'm going to do!" they say, "In fact, I'm going to quit my job right now and tell my boss what a miserable SOB he is!"

Greeting everyone! I am your host Mr. Rourke, and this is my assistant Tattoo. Welcome to Fantasy Island!

Because that's where you are if you believe those things work.

If you want to delve deeper into making money in this manner then get on the email list of those who are really good at it. As mentioned I'm on Alex Becker's list. I am also on Vic Strizheus' list and Mark Dawson's and several others. The reason I am on their lists is because they provide me with information that directly benefits my online businesses.

Here is a list of the top online people according to Forbes magazine

Brian Clark of www.copyblogger.com

Belle Beth Cooper www.buffer.com

Rand Fishkin www.seomoz.com

Michael Hyatt www.MicahelHyatt.com

Avinash Kaushik
https://www.linkedin.com/in/akaushik

Neil Patel http://www.quicksprout.com/blog/

Will Reynolds
http://www.slideshare.net/wilreynolds/presentation
s

Danny Sullivan
https://plus.Google.com/+DannySullivan/posts

Gary Vaynerchuk
https://www.garyvaynerchuk.com/

Keep in mind these people are very advanced and I don't want you becoming discouraged should you visit their site and walk away not having understood a single thing. Remember you're still new at this and there is a learning curve. But in the long run none of it is hard and once you get the hang of it, watching that extra money roll in every month will make you damn glad you didn't give up and were patient enough to follow the steps and master them.

How to Create Landing Pages, Insert Opt-In Boxes, Banner Ads, and other Cool Stuff.

This is where we get serious. You are going to need to purchase some programs and learn a little about how to write and design an ad for your product or service. All of this can be outsourced but I discovered it was less expensive to purchase the products and do the work myself rather than searching for qualified people on fiverr and iwriter. None of this is complex and the products mentioned are worth having.

I know because I bought them, I use them, and they work.

So let's start with the opt-in box. Since I use aweber I will walk you through the process. Almost all autoresponders use the same set up so what I teach here will likely work with get response or mail chimp. However, it may also be a good idea to go to YouTube or Wikihow and in the search box ask how to set up an aweber or Mail chimp or get response account. I find that video tutorials often work better than trying to glean information from a book.

The reason why you need these things is because autoresponders make it possible for you to keep in contact with your customers and maintain a dialogue with them. It lets them get to know you.

But don't overdo it.

I average about 20 business related emails a day. I delete most of them without reading because I'm not interested in being pitched to. If you want me to open your email it had better start off by providing me with something that benefits me.

I'll give you an example. As a writer and publisher I'm always on the lookout for new and inventive ways to increase my readership. With all the free ebooks being offered on Kindle, and a great many of them being terrible, avid readers, the people I very much want on my list, are tuning out and only reading books recommended by friends.

Then I received an email from Mark Dawson in which he claimed to have created a formula that laser targets the avid readers in specific writer's genres AND permits readers to sample your work before they buy. It was a free four video course and one that really opened my eyes to the mistakes I was making marketing my books.

So every time Mark emails me, which isn't that often, I open his email and read it. I have also purchased one of his courses which made it possible for me to supercharge my list of readers. The same applies to Alex Becker and Vic Strizheus. Why? Because the vast majority of emails I receive from them benefit me or my business. If you don't provide value with each and every email, you will be regularly deleted and eventually unsubscribed. Remember it's much easier to keep a customer than it is to get a new one.

With that being said I'm going to show you how to create your first ad, your landing page and opt in box. Now here's how the process works. I'm going to use a Facebook ad as an example because it's the easiest to set up and when done correctly produces excellent results. When you sign up with hostgator also note that they often run free offers like $100 credit in Google and Bing Ads so you may wish to use those as tests to see what works.

Warning* If you use any online ad remember that you will be continuously charged unless you set an EXACT AMOUNT and keep a watchful eye on your ad and how much its costing you. With Facebook they charge you after your ad's end date. To make sure to keep costs under control, purchase a gift card for the full amount you want to spend on ads. Then use that card for ad payments this

<u>way they won't have access to your actual credit card</u>

Okay, so to start find a picture that best represents your product. You can search Google images for something that fits. Size wise it needs to be 1200 pixels wide by 628 pixels long or 4 inches by 2.1 inches. It also cannot have more than 20% in text. Meaning you can't create a 4x2 inch box that states **Buy my excellent widgets! Dead center in big bold letters!** If it takes up more than 20% of the space in the ad, the ad will be rejected.

You can however write copy above and below the picture. Here's an example:

For a **Limited Time** get my **FREE** video course on specialty widgets. See for yourself how they obliterate the competition! **Over 5,000 satisfied customers**. Act now, this FREE course will be selling for $97 dollars this coming

Landing page link will appear here

There are numerous videos on YouTube on how to create a Facebook ad. But to get the most bang for your buck I suggest you watch the videos that show you how to use Power Editor to create one. Power Editor is a Google Chrome feature and can only be used on a Chrome Browser.

Here are the questions you'll need to have answers for

What country do you want to sell to? What state, city or town?

In what language?

Who do you want to sell to, Men or Women or both?

What age range?

What interests? Give some thought to this question. When I place an ad for my book on how to get your book published, in the interest box I type in *writers.* They are my target audience. When placing an ad for this book, I target men not women and only those 45 years to 65+ So ask yourself who will benefit most by getting your product or service? If you're not sure which audience will best suit your needs, you can split test your ads to see which performs better. I'll explain this process later on.

The next step is to create a landing page. You can have this done on Fiverr but you're better off just buying **Instabuild 2.0** and watching the tutorials on how to create the perfect landing page. This is the software program that's the easiest to use, requires no programming skills and provides the best results.

Here's what I do and it works really well. For the picture I purchase an illustration or photo from websites like istockphoto, shutterstock or stockfresh. You simply type in what you're looking for and these sites will show you all the pictures they have on that topic. For example. For my book *Whateverland* I wanted a picture of an amusement park. I went to istockphoto, typed in *amusement park* and after searching for 20 minutes or so I came upon the perfect one. So I purchased and downloaded.

Istockphoto can be expensive so shop around. www.freeimages.com is a good source and you might also check out www.canva.com where you can create just about anything you want for free. And as always you can go to fiverr.com and get someone there to create the ad for you.

Being the creative type I prefer to create the ad myself.

So I went to my adobe photoshop elements program. You can purchase this online at Amazon for under 70 dollars. It's a real timesaver when it comes to creating an ad because you can make whatever necessary adjustments with a click or highlight and erase.

Then I resized the istockphoto and it to Facebook requirements of 1200 pixels wide 628 pixels tall. I also improved the color and sharpness

Then using the textbox I choose the lettering, font, color and size then print on the top of the photo **Whateverland: Paradise or Perdition?** Making sure it didn't take up more than 20% of the picture.

Then I save it to My Pictures

Next step I go to Facebook's Power Editor, fill in the requested information. One of the questions asked is where do you want to send the person who clicked on your ad? The answer is **<u>your landing page</u>**.

With **Instabuild 2.0** the program creates the place where you sell your product. Personally I like to create videos that give a presentation of what I am selling.

I'm going to stop here to explain why I use these programs and to point out that you don't have to.

I'm a writer and as such a creative person. I love writing copy, creating business logos, doing narration and making videos. However if was on your side of this narrative and the author said that in order to make money for retirement I must first learn public accounting, I would immediately say " Nuts to this!" and toss the book in the trash.

So before you think the process is becoming too complex, keep in mind what I'm doing works best for my products and that I love doing it. What you decide on selling or what service you intend to provide might require an ad that is completely different from mine. For example, instead of creating an ad you might choose to do a press release. Press releases work very well in industries that aren't very competitive. Writing and publishing is VERY competitive so they don't perform well for me.

So here again are the products I use to create my ads.

Hostgator to get my domain name and web hosting.

I have Instabuilder 2.0 to create my website for me.

I have Adobe Photoshop Elements 13 to resize the ad photographs to comply with Facebook's ad requirements. This program is the stripped down version of Adobe Photoshop which cost several hundred dollars. The full version is for professional graphic designers and illustrators and contains far more applications than a simple ad or logo will require. Still, the Elements version is fun to use and comes with video tutorials that will teach you everything you need to know. There is also a free program similar to Adobe Photoshop called Gimp. It works well but I found the learning curve considerably steeper than that of Elements.

I also create videos that give a presentation of my products and how my target audience will benefit from them. Perhaps the best place to get started creating presentation videos is http://flixpress.com

This website has several free videos that you can use to give a quick video presentation of your product or service and the best part is that the entire process is cut and paste. It requires no video skills at all!

And it's a lot of fun.

The next step is to create a full video presentation yourself. (Remember you can always outsource this job to fiverr spokespeople.) If you want to do it yourself however, you will need a video creation program. Now before you start thinking this is getting too complex and probably too hard to learn to do let me assure you that it isn't.

Actually it's quite simple.

I use a program called Camtasia studio to create my videos. You can download it for free for about 30 days to try it out. If you like it you can buy it and if not you can delete it.

However if you decide to go forward you will need a microphone. During the free try out period just pick up a cheap microphone for $10-$15 dollars that can plug into your computers USB port.

Here's a quick view of how it works and don't worry, the program has a video tutorial that explains the entire process.

I write down whatever I intend to say beforehand on the notepad program that comes with every computer. Then I go to http://www.Google.com/images and type in the image I'm looking for in the search box. Since this book is about money for retirement, if I was to create a video about this book I would look through Google images to find a group that fits my script.

When you find the ones you like, download them to your computer by right clicking on the image, then scroll down to "save image as…" and click on that. The screen will change and ask you what you want to name the picture and where do you want it kept. I always choose to download it to My Pictures and number them in the order they go into the script meaning retirementpic #1 retirementpic#2 retirementpic#3 and so on.

He's how I create the entire presentation in less than one hour.

NOTE* Don't download a photo that has a name embossed on the center like shutterstock or istockphoto or 123. These are licensed photos and require permission to legally use.

Another Note* Should you decide to fully immerse yourself in online businesses, you will need a professional microphone and headset. Back when I was using a cheap mike and headset, the recording sounded tinny, thin and not at all professional. And I spent too much time erasing pops, clicks and background noise. I presently use a Plantronics wireless headset

**that blocks outside noises well. I bought it at
Staples for about $97 dollars.**

I have discovered (often the hard way) that it's
best to buy the top hardware and software. I
always check the reviews before purchasing so I
know I'm getting a quality product and it will do
exactly what I need it to do.

And now, back to our show.

When you open Camtasia on the bottom of
your screen you will see two rows. The top row is
for pictures or videos and the second is for audio.

I start out by copying and pasting a placeholder
photo of myself or my product or service or
company logo on the video row so the narration
has something to connect to. If your simply doing
a voice over or book narration simply click on
tools and then in the dropdown menu click on
Voice Narration

Here's how my script would read.

Hello, I'm Zackary Richards. If you're like me,
the last few years have been very difficult on your
investments and savings. So what do you do? You
learn how to make money by going on the internet.

Then I go on to say how I did it and how they
can too. I then outline the process by showing how

my product can benefit them and how, by getting it, their lifestyle and income would improve.

Once the narration is complete and all background noises are erased, I start adding photos to the video row when the audio reaches a certain point. For example

Hello, I'm Zackary Richards (Insert picture of myself) If you're like me, the last few years have been very difficult on your investments and savings (insert picture of guy with turned out pockets.) So what do you do? (insert picture of man deep in thought) You learn how to make money by going on the internet. (insert picture of whatever product or service you're looking to sell.) Then go into your benefit list with your product or service proudly featured.

So what do you do when the video is completed and you want to use it in an ad?

The process is simple. Just follow these directions. On the toolbar there is an icon that says produce. Click on that. Then on the next toolbar you will see UPLOAD. This will send you video to YouTube to be uploaded.

<u>NOTE* You will need to create a YouTube account to do this but its FREE and only takes a couple of minutes.</u>

Then when you get to YouTube fill out the information. For example: You will need to name the video and give a description. Like most marketers, start with your websites URL address. then list the benefits that watching the video will offer them. Put in as much information as you can think of. Google likes content and by writing 300-500 words indicates that your video has something to say.

Next under tags you'll want to list keywords that will drive people to your video. But with YouTube you don't use the Google Keyword Planner, you use the Google Display Planner. Here's how to access it.

Go to your usual Google Keyword Planner, and on the top toolbar you'll see the word tools, click on that dropdown menu and click on Display Planner and use it the same way you would use the Keyword Planner.

Fill in the "Tags" box with keywords that have a high number of searches but low competition. They will allow about twenty but usually no more than that.

When the video is finished uploading, click on its location and then watch it to make sure it is what you want. If so, then stop the video at the very beginning. Then under the video, click on

Share. This will provide you with a link to place on your website that will send those who click on it to YouTube to see it.

If you want to place the video on your site and not YouTube's then after you click on Share, scroll down and click on EMBED. Copy the code, then go to your websites dashboard, go to the post or page you want to place the video on, then on the upper right corner click on TEXT. Then paste the EMBED code there.

Once done, click on Update button on the right, then once that is completed, click on view page. And the video should be right there.

I prefer however to create a DVD so I have an actually DVD of the video should I wish to use it outside of YouTube. You will need a DVD burner on your computer to do this.

Insert a new DVD into the DVD drive then with Camtasia, click on *Save and Produce* and then *Where you want it saved*.

The process takes several minutes so don't panic when at first nothing happens. During this process I usually go make myself a cup of coffee and by the time that's done the video is ready to view.

Now here is why this software is so valuable.

What Camtasia studio does is records you as you show how to do something on the computer. Here's what I mean. Say you want to know exactly how I create a book cover for one of my kindle books. Well with Camtasia studio I put on my headset and as I show you the website I use and the process of creating a book cover I explain how I'm doing it and what pitfalls to watch out for.

Basically what it does is permits someone to watch over your shoulder as you do something and records a video of it. For example, I show how to create a book cover on my author site www.zackaryrichards.com

And on my business site www.aricommunications.com I show many of the processes outlined in this book.

This process works for any type of business. It doesn't matter if you're selling informational products like me or gardening hardware. And the big advantage is knowing before you lay out tens of thousands of dollars opening a brick and mortar store whether the business has a good chance of being successful.

I'll give you an example. My daughter and her husband are in the process of opening a vegan restaurant. She lives in a rural area so I was concerned about the difficulty of getting customers. So I invited her over and we sat down and ran through the process of seeing if a vegan restaurant in her area was a good idea.

So we went to Google and typed in Vegan and the area in which she lives. Just as I suspected, there were just a few searches for vegan anything in her area.

However, I begin thinking just *who would be interested* and where would they live? Well, to answer the first question, the people who would likely be interested in dining in a vegan restaurant who be those highly interested in health and fitness.

So I did a search for health and fitness stores in my state as well as gyms. It turns out that a city only forty miles away has a several health and fitness stores as well as a number of gyms.

When I did a Google search for the word vegan in that town, there were several hundred. In addition, there were searches for vegan recipes, vegetarian, and gluten free foods. I also discovered that the main street has several restaurants but none featured vegan or vegetarian fare.

I have also noticed that vegan and vegetarians are very proud of their dietary choices and so I suggested that my daughter and her husband

ALSO offer physical products that are all natural and don't contain any animal products or by-products.

I also suggested that she use the word vegan in the name of her restaurant because of the heavy search volume AND that an exact match domain like veganrestaurant.com would likely rank on the first page of Google for vegan restaurants in that area.

I also suggested that she and her husband create a recipe book for vegans and sell it on Amazon.

Being in the publishing business I can tell you first hand that nothing confirms a person's authority more than by having a book published in their field of expertise.

The next step would be to create a Facebook ad laser targeted toward vegans and offer a lead magnet of their most popular recipe in return for their email address. This way she can survey them and find out exactly what they're looking for. What types of vegan food do they enjoy most and would order in a vegan restaurant? Would they be interested in other products offered for sale like coffee mugs or tee-shirts with the restaurant's logo or would they find that tacky?

By opening a dialogue with the people who would most likely be interested in her product, she can focus all her start up capitol in goods and services her potential customers would be interested in buying.

In the beginning of this book I pointed out how commerce is quickly becoming fully mechanized. As a middle-aged guy odds are you aren't interested in starting a brick and mortar business. Unless, of course, that's something you've always wanted to do but didn't know how.

Well, now you do.

Comedian Chris Rock once told the story of how he started out. After dropping out of school he got a job as a dishwasher in a Red Lobster restaurant. The job wasn't hard, all he had to do was scrape off the dishes, load them into the dishwasher and take them out when they were clean.

But the monotony was killing him. In order to make the day go faster, he decided that he wouldn't check the time for three straight hours. He decide to start at exactly 12 o'clock. He also decided to extend the time he thought each hour would take just to make sure he made it to the three hour mark without checking the clock.

At 12 he began.

He told himself to just focus on the job, keep working and like everyone had told him, when you keep busy time goes faster. So he waited and waited and waited until he was absolutely sure that three hours had passed. He began to feel good, thinking about just how great it would be when he finally looked at the clock and saw it was 3:45 or possibly even 4:15!

So he looked at the clock

1:25

He went on to say, that was the moment he decided he couldn't spend the rest of his life doing that job and any job like it. Knowing he had a talent for comedy, he set out to make himself a career.

And after a lot of hard work, he succeeded.

He explained that with a career, there aren't enough hours in the day. When he checks the clock these days it's a lot LATER than he thought.

And that, he said, was the difference between having a job and having a career.

And believe me I know exactly what he is talking about. I worked in corporate for 25 years. Hated every minute of it. And no, I didn't have to do back breaking physical labor but the drudgery of doing that same task day in and day out made me miserable. As did the daily commute and the getting up at 6:00 am every morning.

Today, I start working at around 10:30 am and often work late into the night. And I don't mind at all. I've always been a night person and I'm at my peek when most people are exhausted and want to call it a day.

So back to the mechanization of commerce.

I was very happy and my daughter and her husband were very thankful that I was able to show them if their business idea had any chance of success. It turns out their original idea would have likely burned through all their startup money and left them with a failed business as well as additional debt.

Master marketer Dan Kennedy makes it very clear in his book *The Unique Sales Page* when he says all businesses are alike.

And that's true, which is why I showed you how to create additional income. The first advantage with starting out online is that you can see beforehand if the product or service niche you've chosen has potential for success.

And if it crashes and burns you're only out about 40 bucks instead of 40 thousand.

Another important point is you learn from your failures. Every successful business man I've ever met had many failures before he clearly saw what would work and what wouldn't. With this book I hope I have decreased the learning curve so that by using the online Google searches and the other steps to see if a product or service with be successful, you'll be ranking in the money in a short period of time.

Here's one nugget of wisdom I discovered that I hadn't realized before I went into business for myself. And it's this: People don't think like me, or you. What you are absolutely convinced with be the best selling product or service ever offered will often be a colossal dud.

That's why it so important to create a mailing list of customers. And to split test your Facebook ads. This way you can find out what they're interested in BEFORE you spend time, effort and money on something that generates tepid interest at best.

Are You Ready to Make Some Money?

In the beginning of this book I pointed out how business is changing and how very important it is for you to create additional streams for your retirement.

However in many cases, people who use the methods I've outlined, discover that they may have something they can build into a full-time, all-in business. The problem is that they don't know how to go about it. That's when you begin looking at entrepreneur forums online and start asking questions.

And one of the questions you should ask is how do I go about crowdfunding my business?

Don't know what crowdfunding is? Crowdfunding is when regular people are made aware of a new venture and are asked to contribute to it.

Here's an example: Over a period of time you have become quite adept at vegetarian cooking and have made a sizeable amount of money selling recipe books on that subject.

You've done well and are now considering opening a vegetarian restaurant but need money for startup costs. So you go to your local bank or credit union and see if you can get a startup/small business loan. The problem is that you are a talented vegetarian chef and not an experienced accountant well versed in business plans and so you are shown the door.

Then you try the Small Business Association (SBA) and although they are open to the idea and might consider loaning you the startup costs, there are numerous hoops, and technicalities and paperwork and wait time that it simply becomes discouraging, so you shelf the idea.

Fortunately things have changed. Now if you have a good idea for a business or simply need money for something people might decide is worthwhile you can plead your case on http://Kickstarter.com or http://Indiegogo.com

So let's go back to our vegetarian chef. You state your case using what is called the four Ps: People, passion, participation and perks.

So let's start with people.

The future of business is all about networking. And the goal of networking is getting to know people and getting them to know you. Facebook, Twitter, Linked-in and YouTube are very powerful when it comes to drawing people together. You can advertise on these sites and laser target your potential supporters.

On Facebook there are over 725,000 people who LIKE vegetarian food. And because vegetarians are a highly motivated group regarding the protection of animals, a request for support of your Indiegogo campaign for startup money for a vegan restaurant might garner considerable financial support.

This goes for the others as well. Plus you can create a YouTube video asking for support and use fiverr.com to promote it and get it to some high volume sites. You then create a Facebook fan page featuring your upcoming business and ask people to like your site. Offer them free recipes and ask what they thought when they made them at home.

Passion—Convince them that you are dead serious about getting your restaurant up and running and that you'll do whatever is necessary to make it a success.

People love success and LOVE to be part of it. Think about that. You contribute $25 dollars and later discover that the campaign was a big success and that as a contributor they are sending you a tee shirt that reads "I Saved an Innocent Life by funding (***name of restaurant here.***)

Feels good doesn't it?

Participation—Ask for help. Find other restaurateurs and ask for input. As long as you're not in direct competition with them I've found that most successful people are more than willing to lend a hand by offering some time and money saving advice.

Perks—First Rule of Business, "What's in it for me?" It's a fair question. If you want me to contribute my hard earned money to your cause, what do I get out of it? I suggest you spend some time on Indiegogo and Kickstarter and see what other people in similar niches are offering. In most cases it's something to do with the product, like a tee shirt or coffee mug or free download.

Here are some helpful hints.

1. **Chose the right project type and let the people know exactly what you want.** For example: I need to raise *x amount of money* by this *date.*
2. **Be realistic when choosing your perks.** If you're asking for $1000 dollars, a coffee mug ain't gonna cut it. As mentioned earlier in this book, find out what works and copy it. You're looking to get funding for a business, not create a new art form.

3. **Tell them your story**—If you want them to give you money, then let them get to know you. Let them know where you come from, why you're determined to get this funding for your project and why you're sure it will succeed.

4. **Give full disclosure**—when people ask questions give honest and direct answers. But, keep the dialogue focused on the funding don't get involved in lengthy discussions not related to topic.

5. **PROMOTE, PROMOTE, PROMOTE!** DO not create a campaign, upload the video and then wait for the money to roll in. Prepare in advance by alerting all your Facebook, Twitter, Linked-in and YouTube subscribers. Write a blog about it and promote heavily. Bottom line, you're not going to get the funding you want if enough people don't know about it.

That's all you need to know to get started. You may need to review this book a few times to know what to do well enough to succeed financially, which isn't hard.

The hard part is deciding to take action and sticking to it until it's done. That's the key to success in any venture, whether it is generating money for retirement, building a business or dealing with life itself.

Persistence and single-mindedness has created more success stories than talent, money or ambition. You *will* run into obstacles, disappointments and set-backs. However, once that positive mindset is established, you'll find a way to win.

Best of Luck to you!

Zackary Richards

You may view other books in the Middle-Aged Man Survival Guide at these locations:
http://amzn.to/1NPIS9k Divorce: The Middle-Aged Man's Survival Guide

http://amzn.to/1KTeMAZ Get Healthy The Middle-Aged Man's Survival Guide.

They are also available as e books and audio books.